Rio Hershey, born in Ohio on a Wednesday in June, has spent most of her life traveling and collecting the tales of others, only to find herself back where she began. After graduating from high school and going on to finish a bachelor's degree from Northern Illinois University, she went on to teach English in any format imaginable to all ages conceivable. From Ohio, to Illinois, to France, Spain, Mexico, Costa Rica, and Saudi Arabia, she is living proof that only the still waters stagnate. "All I know is that I am here until the day I'm not."

To Ms. Mindy Dipietro, Mr. Mark Stevens, and to all of the countless educators whose wonderful minds, kind hearts, and incredible spirits have inspired and encouraged at least one of their students. This book would not exist without you.

Rio Hershey

THE STORY OF NOTHING

AUSTIN MACAULEY PUBLISHERS™
LONDON • CAMBRIDGE • NEW YORK • SHARJAH

I would love to take a moment to thank all of the wonderful people who made my lifelong dream a reality. First and foremost, a special thank you to the publishing team at Austin Macauley, who took the time to review and edit my story. Without them, this book would have never been more than a compilation of online documents hidden on my desktop.

Salma Ali - Thank you for being among the very first readers of my manuscript and giving me the courage I needed to pursue its official publication. You have been my voice of reason and pushed me to strive for excellence from the moment we met. For this and many other reasons, I cherish and value your honesty and friendship.

Shubham Mishra - What is there really to say? You have led by example and have shown, not only to me but to the world, that daring to dream is what makes life worth living. It has been an honor to observe and marvel at our parallelled professional growth. From editing your travel blog to your honest critique of my work, it has been a pleasure learning and growing with you. From the bottom of my heart, thank you for being a wonderful friend and ally.
Finally, a thank you to all of the lovely individuals that I have met on my journeys. This is for each of you—my colleagues, former students, beloved teachers, and the wonderful friends

I have made along the way. Each fleeting conversation, shared laugh, touching moment in shared humanity—each and every one of you has inspired me. Thank you for sharing this life with me, even for the briefest of interactions. While some of us may not remain in contact, know that each kindness has begotten kindness in turn. You are loved and never forgotten.

The Original Sin

What was the original sin?

Adam and Eve in the garden of Eden, and the serpent convinces Eve to eat the fruit from the tree of knowledge. But it is not until Adam partakes in the fruit of wisdom that God intervenes and casts them out. Was only Eve meant to have the knowledge and wisdom – knowing that it was in her nature to share, build, and nurture – and once Adam had a taste, God knew paradise was no longer attainable for mankind on Earth?

Taking a step further back, what if Adam and Eve are a metaphor for the duality of mankind. The positive, giving, building, constructive, and supportive side of humanity, the interconnectedness and inherent kindness we all have in our hearts, being contrasted with the negative, taking, destroying, warlike, selfish, and egocentric side we carry with us. Eve partook in the wisdom, and God knowing it would be used for the betterment of man did not stop nor punish her. It was only when the individualistic, self-serving, self-interested nature of humanity became aware of the same knowledge that God cast us out into a state of nature.

Maybe it is in the original sin that we find the blueprint of life. The interplay of positive and negative, light and dark, masculine and feminine, electrons and protons – life is this constant state flux, instability, and change. The consistent state of inconsistency. Both light and dark partook in the wisdom of the universe, and both have the magnitude for awe-inspiring chaos, whether that be for the betterment or detriment of life on earth. And as we know, we can't have one without the other. Day cannot exist without night as the moon couldn't exist without the sun.

God did not intend for humanity to have the knowledge to manifest and change the course of fate and history. And yet thanks to the serpent, the embodiment of free will, we have the power to create both paradise or hell in our waking day. Is it there that we find our humanity? In the struggle to accept that our inner world is not a stagnant black or white, but a constantly shifting paradox in between the millions of shades of neutrality.

Our Duty to Civil Obedience

Humanity has not changed. Our tools and technologies, yes, but fundamentally we are still in the same mind as our grandparents, our grandparents' great-grandparents even. We talk of change, of wanting to better ourselves but few of us have the courage or desire to make the changes necessary. We sold our souls to institutions that look out for their proper interest rather than our own. We sold our humanity for wealth that can more easily be taken from us than it was to earn.

While we have a duty to hold our governing bodies accountable, our primary obligation and moral responsibility is to ourselves. How are we to determine what is just and unjust for the state when we cannot and do not hold ourselves as individuals to the same standards? When we are content to watch as our neighbor struggles because it is inconvenient for us to lend a hand, but are willing to surrender our income every year in the name of patriotism to furnish foreign wars, why should we expect our government to behave differently? If we want change, it is us, a collective of individuals, who must make the conscious decision to change – to lead by example in our principles.

As Thoreau expounded, "A wise man will not leave the right to the mercy of chance, nor wish it to prevail through the power of the majority."

There is right and there is wrong. There is justice, and there is injustice. However, when the majority is content to sit in the comforts brought to them in systemic facility while others struggle under the weight of its oppressive mechanisms, it is evident that we cannot wait on the placid majority to act. If you desire change, if you desire justice, it is necessary to uncouple this notion that all laws are just and merit obedience.

"If I devote myself to other pursuits and contemplations, I must first see, at least, that I do not pursue them sitting upon another man's shoulders. I must get off him first, that he may pursue his contemplations too." (Thoreau)

When our entire governing body, our entire nation, was built upon the forced labor of others, when our way of life is the fruits of generations of subjugation and injustice, how can we dare call ourselves the land of the free? How are we the home of the brave when the majority is content to sit and watch these injustices continue to unfold and do nothing?

The sooner we realize our true power as a people, remember that the government's power is derived from our consent, the sooner I believe, that we shall witness and embody the principles of liberty and justice for all.

Control

Spinning, spiraling, flashing, bright. Lively, quick, twist, and a stumble. I am not in control… I don't know what is going on… Where are you…

The lights once steady, flash and oscillate, the music comes in and out of focus. My body moving of its own accord. Adrift in the energy, I am scared. I can't steer the ship to shore. We are going to crash. Where are you?

She is here. In the shadows, the corners of my mind. Bubbling deep from within. She is the desire for control in purest form. Her power intimidating me. I crave, no need to feel in control of her at all times. To bury my passions so deep that they cannot hurt anyone. To only be expressed when I say, when I want. To keep her under lock and key and to control the means of expression at all costs.

The opposite of love is not hate… they are two parts of the same whole. The fire that would drive you to sacrifice your life, to risk federal prison and to violate international law. The kind of love that makes you cross seas without hesitation… It is the same passion that destroys lives, foundations. It is the fury that sets the cleansing fire needed to clear the way for rebirth. It is raging, out of control, pushing away and yet coming back for more.

As I have this desire, no, need to feel alive. I cannot deny anymore that my sense of freedom, laughter, joy, grounded in the present moment, wild thunderous, heart-racing passion for life is the very same as the part of me I try to keep buried and hidden. The years of repressed rage, the need to destroy any and all oppressors, to break the chains and to watch the blood run red down their faces. The capacity I have to create and love is equally as deep as my capacity for utter chaos and destruction.

I can no longer embrace one and ashamedly hide the other. Both are necessary to sustain life. As all creatures die and others are born, as the sun sets and the moon rises, I cannot live in this fantasy realm of only creation. Eventually creations grow, evolve, develop, they must pass from one consciousness to another. What no one talks about is that while new growth is beautiful and chaotic in her own splendid way, growth is uncomfortable, painful even at times. It is learning to let go and trust that the process is worth it.

Maybe this is why I feel the need to live a nomadic life. Never stay and form communal roots. In a state of constant arrival and departure, I have managed to live in a state where I have total and yet no control simultaneously. I can choose to leave whenever I feel it is time to move on. I can control where and the means of my journey. However, with each new journey, a new incarnation is formed. The girl who left is never the same woman who returns. Situations and circumstances, new people and new interactions, all shape and help to mold the newest form. She is still the same lump of clay that came into this world. However, through the years, people, and experiences she encounters, each adding, subtracting, twisting, shaping… overtime she slowly morphs into who she is meant to be in that moment. Lessons to learn always, laughter and pain to share. A gentle, reassuring hug that turns into a desperate claw, grasping for a shred of reality while lost in the fog.

The time has come to venture again. Further away from the lighthouse and back into the surf. Still waters stagnate and I choose to be set loose upon the tide. Because no matter how difficult or troubled the past, there is always hope in the uncertainty of tomorrow.

The Tempest

I am everything, and I am nothing
The sand ever-shifting beneath your feet
I am the salt in the air you're breathing
A soft, tender breeze. A sigh of relief
I am the heavens, red at dawn's first light
A sorrowful farewell, the waves they call
Pure enthrallment, impossible to fight
I am your pride, here to destroy you all
Storm clouds gather, hear the rolling thunder
Light fading fast, hope fleeting in its wake
Waves like mountains, poised to pull you under
One final prayer, for there is no escape
I am the sea whose tides carry you home once more
Gently rocking, to wash upon God's golden shore.

The Nymph

Life is for living, *oui*? To breathe in the energy, get lost on the breeze, swept away in the melody of chance. Belonging to nowhere and everywhere, to the present, past, and *future en même temps*. Do not cry for loss but rebel against grief. Dance, drink, make merry – breathe in life and exhale joy. Seek out new horizons, new people, new stories, new adventures. Take delight in the yellow fragrant blossoms, the brilliant blue sky caressing the green canopy of leaves crowning the nymphs below. Pursue passion and fate always follows suit.

As the tide rises and carries the ship to sea, or lowers and runs the crew stranded on land, energy does the same. For those who feel its subtleties pull and push every which way, it manifests in the same polarity. Mania and depression. Infatuation and rage. Enthrallment and disenchantment. Yet in the end, they are simply two halves of the same whole. As roots and the branches below, stretching into the earth – mania is depression reaching out into the world seeking, no, demanding to be inspired by all that surrounds it. Finding enchantment and wonder from the sun and moon above to the February daisy and earth dusted crow below.

Can you not hear the pipes calling? Feel the tambour rattle from within. Get lost in a melody, a rhythm? Feel the pull of destiny dragging your weary soul. If the point is to live, never be sorry for the experiences granted. Simply learn, evolve, and continue along your path. As the shrinking violet can burst through the concrete, you too can withstand and outlast the barriers in your path.

The great lord Pan chasing nymphs. Satyrs as they roam. The simple and weak fear what they only wish to comprehend. It takes a certain amount of bravery, courage, pure madness to have the strength of spirit to live life to its brink. Drink the droplets of joy, eat its fruits from the vines, get lost in the taste of memory, the sensation of its juices slipping past your lips and down your chin. Run through the wilds, into the woods. Let the thorns bite. Simply revel in the sensation of being alive. The good, the bad. The *douleur* and the *douceur*. Simply be. Fire leaping, crackling. The circle of tambours. Feeling the rhythm danced across the goatskin rise from the ground, the vibrations shimmering across the breeze as the very tempo of your heartbeat. One step, two – your hips twisting in time as your arms snake into the darkness. Round the fire, dance its circle. Have the bravery to be the first out there and the endurance to outlast those you've inspired to dance. Lost in a moment, neither here nor there. The leather clad minx and her watery limbs beckoning, the maiden's skirts billowing around her. The black, white, and green twisting, twirling, spiraling around her legs. Gathering the fabric, gaining a running start. Up and over the fire, taking a leap of faith. Singeing her sandals, she sticks the landing. Dust covering her faded blue jeans. Maiden to mother, mother to crone. Rinse repeat. Generations dance to the rhythm of their hands. Twirling, dancing, bending the vibrations of goatskin stretched over the drum to their command.

There is something of the woods. Guarding the past and the future in their eaves – witnessing the maiden drawn to their mystery. There is no one to say yes, none to say no. The only thing she loves more than honor is her own liberty. The forest floor below, the stars above. Yellow blossoms, branches twisting around. The flutes, they beckon along. A clearing. Encircled by trees, protected from prying gaze. A dance. The breeze carrying the salted sea in its wake, the crashing of waves drowned out, no, in harmony with the crackling of fire. A dance. A battle? How easily they mistake her acceptance for weakness. Absorbing his energy just to return, match, entwine. Lost in the moment. In embrace. In something primal, unexplainable. In this moment, whole, she is at her most powerful. That is until she succumbs – allows the chase to end. Oh, you thought you were the hunter, ensnaring your prey. Foolish boy, she knew all along. She saw, calculated, drew you to the clearing. She set it up for you to knock it down. She lined up the perfect shot and left you the arrow to fire. As all dances must, it comes to an end. And off into the night she goes, ethereal, beautiful, entirely unattainable. What? You may have learned her every move, memorized every curve and dip, every dazzling imperfection – but that does not mean you have attained her spirit. For she is the maiden – held to no one's command. Off into the wood, the sun kissing the canopy above. Her curls twisting in the breeze, she blends into the trees. Twirling, spinning, her dress wrapping, encircling her legs. Reaching to the heavens above. As above, so below, our nymph rests. Those curves you so carefully memorized dissolving into the wood. Her serpentine curls the very eaves stretching into the dawn above. She has left you with one task – to prepare for the next chase.

Three Crones

Three crones meet in the depths of nowhere. Each in their hands holds a puzzle to be unraveled, a burden, a treasure. Beneath these eves, in the fading light of today, each has come to confess. Confide.

Their stories weighing them to the earth, keeping them from soaring to the heights they otherwise could have achieved. The assumed guilt internalized – the shame, the rage suppressed for so long it ate each from within. Each bearing a story, a lesson in their wake.

The center crone approaches, each step placed with purpose and care. Her watery eyes find mine. In her gaze I see a reflection of myself. Mirrored images of shared trauma and internalized shame. Her perfectly crafted mask appears to have finally cracked. In defeat she removes the painted porcelain to reveal her own humanity.

She steps closer, gaining confidence with each step. She turns the mask over in her hands, marveling the braided lines of silver and blue. Setting its weight softly at my feet, the crone rises. She draws in closer, pulling me into an embrace. Broken, barely audible, she breathes, "I believe you. Do you believe me?"

The weight of her words holds me fast. Turning my blood to lead. She looks into my eyes, searching for understanding, forgiveness. Pulling her close I reply, "Of course I believe you."

The crone smiles. The words she had searched for, craved for so long, finally released into the world. Set free she wanders into the sunset, her white skirts dancing with each step.

The second crone approaches in the fading light. Draped in her own discontent, she draws her dark mantle closer. She maintains her distance, unsure of my intent. After pausing to examine her surroundings, the third crone standing back, she sets a box to the forest floor. Ornately carved with a rusted heart shaped locket, she hands me the key.

"Locking yourself away to avoid pain is an exercise in futility. You will ultimately hurt yourself far worse than anyone else possibly could."

Turning on her heel, the second crone is swallowed into the darkness enveloping the wood. Her shawl the night sky, ushering in the rising of the moon.

Silver light descends upon the clearing and I feel our time is drawing to a close. The third crone still stands there. Silent sobs seizing her, shoulders heaving in grief. Her cries fill the night.

She pauses a moment. Her eyes, vividly blue and red, the crone steps forward and takes my hand. Together, alone in the dark, she recounts tales of love and loss. Of heartache and joys. Of those who left and of those who in death always remain.

Wiping away her tears she slowly shakes her head. Reaching under her cloak of grey, she reveals a small mirror.

Holding it to herself, she allows me to see its reflection. Hazel eyes pierce through the dark. Passion, rage, betrayal fill the air between her and the man looking at us through the mirror. The crone closes her eyes and the man vanishes. Upon their reopening, a different visage appears. Doey brown eyes weepily smile through the void. The crone looks away once more into the night.

"I have taken on the mantle of others for so long. Their hopes, joys, and sorrows. Their expectations and mores. For so long I have taken on their visages, I can no longer find my own."

The crone gingerly places the mirror in my hand, and wearily smiles. With a nod, she takes the path trailing behind me. Alone with mask, key, and mirror, the weight of their words diffusing into the night, I turn my smile inward. For I know with each confession, they have finally set themselves free.

Mountain

Air growing thinner, quickening my pace
The summit lies ahead, just out of sight
Birds in the eves, flies trapped in spider's lace
The sun, my soul, my passion burning bright
Don't look back now to the thicket below
To the paths taken in misdirection
Listen to the tempest, heed its bellow
Darkening skies, honing imperfection
Is this conviction a vice or virtue
This maddening need to realize fate
Upon the plateau, will my sight be true?
Or once again, my dreams left to stagnate?
Alas, to be human is to be shortsighted.
These are the foothills, my efforts unrequited.

Intuition

Moonlight caressing all she touches. Her eyes – piercing, intimidating, enthralling – pools of jaded optimism beckoning me forward. The wind encircling us, tresses of black twisting their serpentine dance. She calls to me.

Onward into the wood. The next tale ready to be conceived. In the realm of shadows and danger lurking beyond my vision, she is my guide. Though I sense that not even she, the goddess always beyond my grasp, beyond my comprehension, fully knows the way herself. All that there is, all that will ever be, is an unspoken bond. A mutual understanding that as long as I place my trust, my future, my very existence, into her snowy hands, I will be kept safe and lead to where it is I must go. It is in this moment, surrounded by the shadows of doubt and the fleeting time of the present, that our fingers entwine.

Roots contrive to trip me, branches grasping my arms, attempting to hold me in my place. The present a reminder of my sins and trespasses. Maternal and ethereal, her quiet disappointment is a reminder of our bond.

And yet, a seed of doubt persists. This tale, this adventure, this voyage of self-discovery – is it nothing more than escapism guised as tenacity?

Is my urge to travel beyond the limits of my comprehension, to expand my horizons – is it a manifestation of an outdated and cyclical coping mechanism? My entire existence I have wanted nothing more than to flee. To outrun the troubles that seek to drown me in the depths of their dread. I have tried out running them before. To distract from the overwhelming shadows by seeking pleasure in ignorance. And to no surprise, the less aware I was, the more power I had unwittingly surrendered to the shadows.

Somber, demure, pure force of will and enchantment – this otherworldly spirit has always been at my side. Watching me torment myself until I was finally ready to accept her embrace. Though coming to terms with our arrangement has proven difficult, she has maintained her promise. Neither she nor I care to surrender our strength. Come to terms with our vulnerability.

I look up from the forest floor and we lock eyes. Her freckled nose and oceanic eyes betray her sentiments. Her lip curled in a snarl, her eyes flashing with the phantom pain of loss. Blue, gold, and green, her eyes reflect my own. In that singular moment, I no longer saw my ethereal goddess, but myself. Before I could formulate a thought, all snapped into place. Those large watery eyes returned to their original depths, her snarl an inward smile, the freckles danced away and left the same glowing angular visage I have come to know.

Tu es amoureuse de lui?

The truth being, I am incapable of love until I heal myself.

Grasping my hand tighter, she pulls me, forcefully, into the unknown. She is my guide, my intuition. She is the voice that quietly tells me to take the risk. The voice that screams at me to rise again. She is all that I have.

And so we walk, hand in hand, through the wood. Into the very shadows I have sought to evade for so long. The silver of the moon radiating from her, my only source of light into the abyss.

Mania

Unyielding. Immoral. Magnetic.

Playing your weakness while hiding her own. Hunting purely for pleasure, for sport, destroying all in her wake. She doesn't love you, or more so she is incapable for she doesn't know how to love in the first place. Hiding behind her bravado, a little girl in mommy's heels, she dances you away. Swept in the chaos, the allure of her charm, you never see the cliff she is dangling you over. Leaving you to fall, alone, the scent of her lingering as you hit the ground. Your heart is scattered to the wind, along the ground, everywhere but in your chest. It belongs to her now. And yet, she doesn't want it. For you were too weak. You should have known better than to play her game. To take the risk. You should have known better than to trust her outstretched hand and to dance in the first place. She warned you, didn't she?

"I'm only going to break your heart in the end. Are you sure of this?"

She knows who she is, through and through. Cruel, calculating, captivating. The harshness she uses as a shield is the very web that traps her prey. It was never her intention to be like this. Deep down she wants to follow you off the cliff. To fall, wrapped in your embrace. Or better, to take the fall and to have someone at the bottom to catch her. But it will never happen. Instead, she exacts her revenge upon the innocent.

Wielding the knife instead of protecting her from the pain it inflicts, she learned to trust no one. Disappointment by disappointment, lie for lie, each abandonment a brick that builds the wall she so desperately tries to scale.

All that remain are the scars. The cuts on her hands, reminding her of the wasted efforts. She is safer here, hidden behind her wall. Safety in her solitude. And yet, the web is spun, the line cast. She tempts her prey with the promise of mystery. Her vulnerability a prize to be won. And yet, she wants for once to play prey. To be chased. For some fool to be brave enough to get caught in her web, to scale the wall she built, to prove that even a waste of life such as herself is even worth the effort it took.

Lies. Fantasy. All their efforts are in vain. Everyone has shown they cannot survive her crucible. Each failure adding yet another brick to the wall. Each disappointment increasing the difficulty on the next attempt. In her sobriety, she knows her game and attempt to save her prey from herself. Hiding in her fortress, she knows better than to let any light shine through its windows.

There she goes, drinking in life. Each sip draining the caution from her. Lost in her own madness, she simply doesn't care. They are grown, let them fall. They know better. She is out to live, to drink every last drop and profit from every golden moment. Laugh, give her the attention and affection she so craves. Let her refill her own glass from yours – draining your affections until she tires of you. Taking your hand, blinded by her smile, lost in the depths of her eyes. You are not much longer for this world. Her mania looks like heaven. Her madness resembling an infatuation with life. The magnetism of the void pulling you in. It is not your fault. Even she does not know the full strength of the power she wields so carelessly, so recklessly. And so you go, hand in hand, spiraling out of control. Only one will survive. And it won't be you. It was never meant to be you. You were a pawn in her game. She was never meant to cultivate sentiment. She was to remain like marble. Cool, unreachable, fragile yet hard. Yet here she is, sacrificing herself again for the unworthy, praying her martyrdom may account to something someday.

The woman behind the mask. The hero in every fairytale, she rides to rescue everyone. From the tiniest mouse to the loudest shriek, she rides to save the day and refuse the credit. It was never her's to have. Only a god you refuse to believe in can save you now. And so you ride. Harder, longer, further into the unknown. Running from the pain. The shame. The humiliation that you are simply unlovable. Unapproachable. Inhuman. Mistakes, missteps magnified beyond their means.

Lock the door, hide the key. She is safer here. Locked in her fortress, she is nestled in the tower, above the *quotidienne* muck. No one goes searching, and she can rest comfortably in the security of incertitude. It is in the shadows she has found grace. If beauty is in the eye of the beholder, then vice is just virtue by another call.

Giving a Voice

Red, blue, green, yellow. Red, blue, green, and yellow. One by one, counting the multi-color lights. Rocking myself to sleep, wondering if I would ever be enough. In the moment I just accepted the fault, even now I try to rationalize. Everyone makes mistakes, everyone is human, the world doesn't revolve around me. And yet, why is it the six, seven, eight, thirteen-year-old girl having to play the adult?

"You know how she is. Just play nice, be the bigger person."

But Dad, isn't she the adult? Why do you let her get away with this? Why do you never believe me? Why don't you care enough… What did I do wrong?

All I have wanted was just an ounce of your attention. To finally be worthy of your praise. Instead, I have internalized your absence as my lack of effort; my deficiencies. Even now working through this, understanding that I was just a child, knowing better… there are still nights I question what I could have done better. Did I not work hard enough? Did I not achieve enough for you?

You said it yourself, the only way to make you proud was "not to be a slut like your mother".

I am trying to grow. Move on. Accept that others have had it worse and my past has only strengthened me.

That doesn't take back nor negate the sleepless nights. The flashbacks of watching you hold her by her throat, shove her son and break his tooth. It doesn't stop me from remembering the sensation of sailing through the air only to crash into the wall. It doesn't stop the depression and anxiety – the constant need to overachieve because if I dare rest for one moment, lose my sense of utility to others for even a second – I have no value or worth.

I am terrified to let anyone close from the years of being lied to and emotionally manipulated. Just when I thought I could rely on you, you ran off again. Abandoned me when I needed you most. Where were you when she rationed toilet paper while I was in grade school? Where were you when she kicked me out of the house for two weeks right before the start of seventh grade?

Oh, that's right, you were too busy sleeping with whatever coworker you managed to talk into bed with you. What? You didn't think I would realize as an adult looking back, that you took me with you to your little soirees when I was five or six? Leaving me in some woman's living room while you went upstairs to "help her with some paperwork". Or all of the times you would point out attractive younger women when it was just us? What was it you said, "The older you get the more disgusting I feel?"

Oh, did you think I was going to forget your transgressions? Throwing a full pack of pads at my head because me starting my period was an inconvenience to you and your wife. The countless meals you ruined while I was away at my mother's – how could I forget being a literal child and consistently reminded of what a disgusting pig I was. That I should be dieting and watching what I eat.

The only happy memories I have of you are in the car, singing along to music. It was the only way I was ever able to bond with you. Those precious car rides being exchanged between you and Mom, Garth Brooks and Duran Duran. Every time I hear *Cruel to be Kind* by Nick Lowe, I hear your raspy falsetto. Or those errands we would run when your wife wasn't with us. The laughter shared, the miles passed.

You had spent years telling me that you wanted a relationship with me. That you didn't want us to end up like my mother and her father. And yet, for as long as I can remember, you have placed any and all responsibility onto my shoulders.

I have spent the first twenty years of my life walking on eggshells and praying that one day I may be worthy enough of your affection and attention. Only now do I see that I always was worthy. It was you that hid in self-indulgent behaviors and playing the victim as a means to avoid responsibility for your own healing.

I will never get that time back. The years I had convinced myself that everyone would be happier if I was never born. The years I had convinced myself that I was unlovable and would die alone. The countless nights I had spent crying myself to sleep because the six-year-old self could not understand why her dad and his wife didn't want her around.

I hope maybe in validating what had happened, that by giving a voice to the inner child that has been forced into silence for so long, that maybe I can begin to heal and truly embrace the woman I am meant to be.

Trapped in Memory

Mouth agape. Eyes to the heavens. A scream so powerful, mournful, all-consuming that it seizes in her throat. Silence. All here has or ever will be. Her arms crossed, ensnaring one another, squeezing tighter and tighter. Just to verify that she is in fact real. Breathing. Alive.

Another argument. A raised voice, a slam of the door. Heavy footsteps, heart quickening. Panic. What is it this time? Or has there ever truly been a reason. The sound of the door unlocking, thudding of a dish onto the counter, silverware clanging in the sink… all foreshadowing the next event.

And yet, male dominance is asserted by the grasp of the wrist. No, not grasp, the tightening of fingers, pinning your arm to the wall. Denying your right to leave. Cornered, pinned, thrown, trapped. Sailing through the air, crashing into the wall. Attempted exit, forced to the wall, only then to be angrily discarded.

Cough Syrup

"You're a piece of shit like your mother and that's all you'll ever be."

The women hidden in the grains of wood, rose tinted globe on the ceiling, the ever-obnoxious yellow carpet, and back again. Face down in a sea of faded blue fleece. This is my home. My life. Despite my best I am never good enough. Never will be. I am the cause of everything wrong in this household. I am the reason Mom and Dad fight so much. I am the reason my brother cries and bites me. Everyone would be happier if I were to just die… no one would miss me. In fact, everyone's lives would be better had I not been born… I look around for an escape, but there is none. And so I write this note, one time, three times – I'm sorry. Each time I fail to escape. And I pray. I pray for the wisdom just to survive another day with no end in sight. And in the moments where I am ready to give up – where I slice my wrist, let the blood rush to my head, drinking the entire bottle of medication – she is there. My goddess.

Love, please no. You have a bright future ahead of you. Just hold on. There are people who love you. Your mother loves you. Don't do this.

Her blue eyes watering, the short blonde curls framing her luminescent face. She frowns. Not in disappointment, but a deeper, almost pitying sentiment. And each time I ignore her.

*"Why do you want to leave – huh? What have I done to you? I have supported you, provided for you – what has she done? Yet you go running off to her? You can't even give me a few more months to find a job working from home? I have looked after you yet you can't give me two months? She's a piece of trash just like her mom, what did you expect. **Little Lisa** – Unfucking believable. I have been there for you! Remember the time she tried to rip you from my arms? When she almost hit my son in the head, yet you choose her. You don't fucking care about me, or any of us!"*

One cup, two cup, three or more cups of whiskey – my father yelling in the doorway. I prayed for sleep. Hid in my silence. Hoping that if I said not a word, he would tire himself out and leave me to my self-loathing fueled nightmare ahead. But no. The barrage continued. For hours. There was no escape. Finally, after two hours – an eternity – he grew tired of yelling and stormed off, slamming the door behind him.

I broke. Completely. The tears streamed down my face in a torrent of hopelessness and despair. I truly was the cause of everything wrong. Every plight and moment of suffering cast upon this family began with me. It was entirely my fault – because I exist. I am the square peg trying to shove myself into the round hole where I clearly do not belong. I am the black sheep grazing among the snowy flock.

The codeine cough syrup. Sitting up on the shelf, it calls to me. Promising the sweet kiss of slumber. A final escape from the hell I could never escape.

She appears to me once more, my goddess. Tears gently sliding down her snowy cheeks. But I no longer care. All I can feel is this desire to be set free – by the bottle. Twisting off the cap, I hold onto its square, rectangular shape, looking down the eye of my savoir. Before I can conjure a thought to the contrary, I take four large gulps – the cold liquid sliding down my throat – the promise of eternal slumber beckoning me to cry myself into its depths once more.

Then I woke up. To the sunlight streaming through my window, and a heaviness in my soul. Knowing my *séjour* in hell did not end in my sleep. That I must face my tormentors anew.

Years have gone by. And it strikes me anew. The feeling of hopelessness. That I am powerless. I see her. The little girl with her face down in the pillow. Unwanted. Unloved. For no other reason than misplaced envy. Filled with rage – all I want is to build a wall around her. Shield her from the evils outside of her door. Yet there she is with the knife. The letters. No one to ever know or read because just as defending herself is a further sign of disrespect, her vulnerability and weakness are weapons to be used against her. I can feel the tears slide down my cheeks as I feel the emotions anew. Raw. Being forced to put my schoolwork second to tend to my brother who was encouraged to abuse me. To take years of being told I am a self-absorbed piece of shit who will never amount to anything. The only way to gain approval was not *to be a slut like your mother*. That I am nothing, was nothing, and that I will never gain the acceptance I sought so dearly. I see her again, still prostate – angry tears staining the pillow. Being ridiculed for situations she was forced into.

Please love. Hold on. Just a bit longer. You are better than this. You will find the love and acceptance you seek. I love you; your mother loves you. You are a strong woman who can conquer anything you seek to accomplish. Just please, sweetheart, hold on.

Then I see her. My goddess, my vision. Her blonde curls and sorrowful, concerned gaze. Eyes that vaguely resemble mine.

In the end, was I not my own savior? The woman holding me close at eleven and twelve years of age, my guide, my hope… I look at the moment in retrospect and see not a goddess… but an ethereal version of my current being.

Is the lesson of a decade in the making hiding in the recesses of my memory? Whether this is a god, gods, or no, that in the end only we can save ourselves. Ultimately no matter what stage of life, it is our own choices in times of despair that shape us into who we are. I was the voice of love, light, and laughter that my younger self needed when all she knew was shadows and chaos. And now, the mere reflection of it all is enough to remind me of my journey – where it began in the abyss of nothing to wherever the path may lead.

I cannot change what has been done. I cannot change the sorrows I have been forced into facing. Yet, these moments of chaos have shown and guided me to where I need to be. These branches, twisted in the dark night turned out to be the rope through the labyrinth leading me towards the inevitable, and for that I am grateful.

The Woman from Nowhere

You can run. But you can't hide. Up there in your castle – unblemished. Untouchable. Seemingly unreachable. But I know. You know. God knows what you have done.

I pray that you look deep into the mirror and are swallowed whole by your reflection. That everything you have put me through reaches out to grab you by the throat. To throw you at the wall as you did me. To leave you battered, bewildered, alone. Trapped in the four corners of your own hell with no escape. I pray your every action is met with equal retribution.

There was a time when all I craved was your validation. A plant withering in the heat of your dismay. But as we have come to learn, no matter how much the grass prays, the sun is too distant to acknowledge the existence of a single blade, nor notice its suffering.

I have spent my whole life trying to make you love me, only to realize the only thing you have ever loved is your own ambition. That fact alone haunts me to this very day. Why was I never enough? Too much? Why did you let her torture me? Why did you choose to sit and watch while any ounce of happiness or individuality was crushed under her heel? So you could swoop in and play hero only when it suited you? Oh wait, to be a hero you would have actually had to do something. Instead, you just sat there, told me to be the bigger person. To play nice.

Your wife endured enough by your hand and then took it out on me. You chose to cultivate her resentment and in turn she humiliated me, loathed my very existence. How dare you claim to have loved me. That I was the only reason you have to keep living. As for your wife – I hope, I pray – I hope she endures every bit of pain and suffering she has put me through. You both think you are untouchable – moving away, out of reach, out of mind. But the truth always finds a way. Both of you will pay dearly for your sins against the innocent.

You robbed me of a childhood. Robbed me of my passions, my happiness, my personality. You robbed me of family and love. You brought me nothing but misery and years of suffering that I can never get back. When all I wanted was to feel included, to feel like I had family, at every turn I was instead reminded that I came from nothing, that I am nothing. That I wouldn't amount to anything. Just another mouth to feed. Instead of building me up, you chose to tear me down. My dancing was too loud, the violin was awful. I was lazy, ignorant, a show off, a wannabe. I was ugly, annoying; my presence tolerable at best.

I was a prize to be won. And once you stole your trophy, you locked it away. Kept it safe at all costs. But the thing you seem to forget is that I am a person, not some doll to be thrown in the corner and talked to whenever you need your ego soothed. I am a person. I am your daughter. Yet who was there to soothe my spirit after I wrote my first suicide note at the age of ten? Not you. Who was there to talk me out of drinking the bottle of cough syrup only to be met with disappointment and the grey dawn when it was death I longed for? Not you. In fact, you were too busy reminding me of what a selfish, useless, pathetic waste of oxygen I was. Who was there through the nights of screaming, yelling, being punched and kicked? Not you. But do you know who was there? Me.

I picked myself up after every attempt to end my suffering. I was the one who pushed myself to achieve greater and more daunting heights. I was the one who soothed the inner child whose only wish was to be held and to feel loved.

Every disappointment, every short coming you had as a man, as a father, I had to pick up the slack. Thanks to you kidnapping me and taking me away from my mother, I was forced to fulfill her role as well. I am the child, the father, the mother. I am the girl with her stuffed animal crying silently to sleep. I am the teenager praying for death by circumstance and recklessness. I am the woman holding them close, thankful and heartbroken to have survived it all.

I am the woman from nowhere. But more importantly, I am the spirit you could never break. I survive in spite, to be the light that illuminates your sins. To be the lantern that guides other lost and battered souls like mine to paradise.

We Are Trees

We are trees. Some saplings, some hundreds of years old. And yet we all face the same struggle for truth and knowledge.

Some of us choose to go to our roots, the physical. Explain the world using science and technicalities, exploring physical avenues to explain our existence. Some choose to explore our branches, each religion and its variants. Looking for God and a higher power.

Yet does not each branch, despite extending in completely different directions, resemble one another? And does not each root, gnarled and stretched into the Earth, growing in opposing ways, do they not all perform the same functions?

Doesn't the canopy of interlaced branches resemble the tapestry of roots below? So why is it that we try to claim our branch is the only true branch and the only way to reach the sun? And why would the branches above condemn the roots for living in darkness, when without their connection into the physical, the tree would be without stability, without life.

We are the trunk – needing to branch higher, searching for wisdom and warmth above, while connected to the physical below. What bothers me is this idea that we are disconnected from our fellow plants, our fellow trees. When one tree falls in the forest, doesn't fungi grow upon it to aid in decomposition? When one sapling is lacking in nutrients, doesn't the mature oak to its left share via the roots below? When one tree is sick and diseased, doesn't its illness infect those around it?

That which uplifts others uplifts ourselves, and that which harms those around us by extension will harm the individual as well. So I ask again, why do we refuse to acknowledge this spirit of interconnectedness? While one tree may grow gnarled and bent and another upright and tall, do we not all need and deserve the same water and sunlight to grow?

All of the branches reach towards the heavens, and all of the roots sink into the earth. Yet we need both, regardless of which direction our roots twist or which way our branches face, to sustain our growth and survival.

When we strengthen our roots, our sense of community, we create a solid foundation from which we all may continue to reach greater heights.

The Freedom in Surrender

From north to south, to the east and west. Trailing, spiraling into one another. These knots, these cords flowing seamlessly… If this is time, and we have had to fragment it for our own comprehension, are we truly understanding? Time, fate, destiny, none of it is linear. As the serpent glides through the glade, the river meandering through the wood only to turn unto itself once more, to follow the path of least resistance. Why is it human nature to try to confine, to limit, to control these things? As we raise levees, the rain waters will always flood once more. As we straighten the rivers, do they not overflow their banks eventually?

Maybe this is the original sin. The unyielding urge to control, to tame, to possess. To claim ourselves masters of another's domain. Only when we realize that it is impossible to reign supreme, to truly be a master of one's destiny. Only when do we surrender to the push and pull of fate are we finally set free.

This is why many fear death.

Death, dying, returning to the earth from which we came, it is the only guarantee in this world. It is the one thing everyone knows we cannot control, cannot possess, cannot predict. Which is why so many fear its approach, its arrival.

The human condition is to build a life based upon reflection into prior experience – to anticipate a future that will probably never materialize. Yet when we let go of the future, realize that based upon the past and present, that there is no sense nor desire to imagine a distant tomorrow, when we surrender to the unknown and accept our lot – that is when we are set free.

That is not to say that we should give up on our dreams. It is to say instead of straightening the river, changing its course to best suit where we will it to go, we should follow its curves. Trust the twists, the turns, the changing of the current, the shallow channels, and hold confidence that water knows where it is meant to go.

Are we not all made of water? The waters of the womb that carried us into this world, the water in our veins that sustains existence, the sweat on our brows, our tears of joy – as the river flows without question, as the tide rises with the moon, yielding to the push and pull of the universe is our natural state of being.

We are everything and nothing. Subatomic particles stacked upon one another, a twisting trail of genetic code. A consciousness trapped in flesh, blood, and bone. And yet still, aren't most atoms 99.9% empty space?

The space between electrons and protons, negativity and positivity, the silence surrounding the noise, what if this is the ebb and flow of divinity itself? Ever present and dictating how our spirals trail, how the rivers meander, how the vines twist and the circle of life keeps turning... What if this silence is that which we can't control, the living energy of all?

Maybe the human condition is to acknowledge the presence and in the face of its awful power, to choose ignorance. Willful ignorance, perhaps arrogance. That we are stronger than its pulls and pulsations. And yet is it not blasphemous to claim ourselves greater than God? To claim ourselves the strongest force in the universe?

What if God is not dead, but within and surrounding us.

To Live

Many choose to spend a lifetime not living. This is perfectly acceptable as a choice. Expectations are met, boundaries in place. There is a clear sense of direction and duty. Right and wrong. What happens when we choose to live?

What happens when we grow tired of living in the fog of our imposed reality. When the expectations of society, of family, of religion; when the expectations of work, of output exceeding at a growing, cancerous rate; when the leak turns into a flood of noise that consumes us, do we simply surrender? Is surrender truly easier than breaking these chains?

If success is found in losing myself to the machine – filtering and grinding myself to nothing against the expectations of outside structures, then maybe, I choose not to be successful. Or rather, I refuse to allow my worth to be measured by someone else's standard.

And so, what happens when we embrace our authenticity? To find what it means to live measured in moments rather than dollars? When we finally learn what it means to be happy in our own company?

In the end, we are only ever truly accountable to ourselves. The choices we make, the consequences of our actions. To be happy is to live a life where we can accept our choices. Where we harbor no regret, guilt, or shame in our decisions. If we can continue forward, not weighed down by our actions, then maybe that is what it means to live a life well-spent.

When we are happy in our own company, can find joy in the rising of the moon, marvel at the expanse of our universe in the stars above; when we can find joy in surrendering to our passions and to childlike wonder, are we ever truly alone? When we base our worth and measure our happiness by our own standards, the people we allow in our lives can only add, never subtract.

I refuse to surrender to the ether once more. To filter myself until all that remains is the dust of who I once was. To embrace yourself in its entirety, in its authenticity, is to embrace life, and I choose to live.

Lightning

Do we truly know when lightning will strike?

Where?

We understand the condition necessary, the buildup of energy.

But that precise moment it all releases in violent harmony, remains a mystery to us all.

Some stand with a metal rod for hours, hoping for inspiration, only to have their efforts unrequited. Perfectly unscathed. While there's some of us who go through life minding our own, only to be struck unwittingly upon several occasions.

Everything amounts to nothing and yet, nothingness is everything.

We are all nothing, occupying carbon vessels. Waiting for lightning to strike and form us into something new. Yes, lightning is more often to strike when you are prepared with a metal rod, wielding your ambition. Oftentimes however, it is the unplanned that is the most impactful.

I cannot shake my fist at the sky, argue with God, force change upon the land. I can feel the tension building, static growing, but it is not I who decides when ideas become reality.

It is an honor to brew in this primordial stew. Taking on the flavors of the world around me. Giving and receiving, exchanging notes and tones. I am but one instrument in a symphony of noise, a caucus of catastrophe. We each have our roles to play, our lines to be sung. Our specific yet integral flavor to add to this mess we call a stew.

We are not the cook. The one who stirs the pot. The one who will inevitably turn down the heat and put an end to our seemingly ceaseless circling. We are born of nothing and like that return to nothing. Just waiting for transformation in between.

Breaking the Surface

Breaking the surface, the frozen tide overriding my senses. Shards of pain, icicles in my blood, enveloping me in a comfortable numb. Diving deeper and further into the unknown. Darkness, confusion, and yet this all too familiar stillness. Further we go, lost in the spiral of memory. Does she miss me? I still see her waving from the shore, serpentine curls twisting in the wind. Those sharp, piercing – icy, frigid, harsh and entrapping – terrifyingly deep pools of mist calling me home. Her perfume fills my lungs, my ears, her sultry voice. I forget how to breathe… Oh wait, that is right, the rope around my ankles. Almost forgot I had ankles, or a body rather. My darling, I tried to return to you and your warm embrace. Despite my efforts, the miles, the battles won and lost, the paths paved and stories spun, I find myself here – Looking up to the curling crescent moon and a rickety boat rocking in the surf. Downward lies the cement block drawing me home, and to you once more. My dearest, against all odds I did return to your shore. Searching high and low, every street carrying whispers of your name. When finally our eyes did meet once more, were you in the arms of someone I knew before. Only now do I see, returning to the reality of the sea welcoming me to her depths, that my heart belongs with her.

For it is she, the brine that is the love of my life, that finally sets me free.

51

Wolf in Sheepskin

I do not pretend to know why I am here.

Nor do I pretend to know my purpose, my goals, my aims nor my ambitions.

I am nowhere and everywhere. At peace in the unknown. Comfort in knowing my heart and trust in the present.

My heart has been caged, restrained. A madman shackled to its environment. Too much, never enough, the odd bits poking out where they shouldn't. Shoved and pressed into molds it was never meant to take. Convinced the problems derived from my shortcomings and malformed reality.

Upon removing the restraints do I find the problem wasn't to be found in this perceived ferocity. In its truest state of docility, I find the cage was never there to protect others from my savagery, but rather to maintain a state of constant utility.

How strange it is to find the acceptance that I have fought for in a state of surrender. How peculiar this juxtaposition – my presence welcomed even when I have done nothing to earn the hospitality.

I do not pretend to know when or how the chains slackened. Nor do I claim to know their origins.

What I do know is this – there is more empowerment in the Shepard's shadow than there ever was pretending to be the wolf in sheepskin.

The Storm

Trapped in a downpour, somewhere between here and there. Miles ahead, miles behind. Debris crosses my path, cars pulled to the side. It is in this moment of ironclad determination where others wait to let the storm pass that I press onward.

I can barely see the road ahead of me, yet I continue. The wind tossing me left and right, the rain falling in obscuring waves, and yet I trudge ahead. The ever-faint line marking the edge my guide, the deluge a reminder of the precarity of my situation.

It is in these moments, trapped between yesterday and tomorrow, that I remember my strength. There is no questioning what if, no contemplating what should have been. Only now. And now, against all odds, all forces of nature, all reason, I obstinately traverse the storm.

Wide-eyed, jaw set, white-knuckled, I face the road ahead. I know what lies on the other side, I know what must be done to reach it, and nothing, not even the wrath of Mother Nature and God himself, are capable of preventing me from seeing this journey to its end.

Grasping at a Memory

Seeping from every corner, the memories cascade and drown my senses. Sliding down the walls, I see our efforts to hang the paper – you on your toes, reaching to the ceiling. Underneath the wallpaper in the living room is our writing – scribbling calculations on the old yellow paper. Under my toes, the carpet we laid, pressed into the corners. In the kitchen I see the washing machine I helped you to install – the memory of its shock still passing through my fingers. I see the fridge and the stove we picked out together. I see the star on the window that I put up for the holidays. The same star that you've left hanging months later as a reminder of me. In the living room I see all of the meals we've shared, the nights we've slept on the floor, the innumerable conversations. I see the night I went too far and despite it all, you still took care of me. On the balcony I see us – hanging the line and all of the times we hung the wash upon it to dry. A life we shared, finding beauty and joy even in the seemingly mundane.

In the bedroom I see us. Your sleepy morning smile, the way your eyes crinkled with laughter. I see every night we made love, a string of lights casting a warm glow across your face. I see every disagreement, argument. Every compromise and apology. I see our goodbye before I parted for America for the first time. Not wanting to leave your side, even if only for a few weeks. I see all of the times I left thereafter because I was scared and pushing you away. I also see each time you took me back, the courage to never lose faith in me.

In the doorway there is us, wrapped in a never-ending embrace. Crying tears of joy to be reunited once more. Not wanting to, refusing, to let you go. Hardly believing it was really you in my arms. The scent of your cologne lingering still in my memory. I see us dancing in the kitchen, dancing in the living room, dancing in the bedroom. Your arms holding me tight, swaying to the music.

In everything in this apartment, everywhere I look, I see you. Us. Our story.

Wrapped in this bittersweet melancholy, I am not ready to say goodbye. I am not ready to lock the door one last time and place the keys in the mailbox.

I am not ready to say goodbye to you.

Une vie sans toi est un monde sans soleil. C'est la mer sans l'eau. Une vie sans toi est un livre douloureusement vide.

My heart is breaking at the thought of leaving the first place that has ever felt like home. But I guess that is life. To find family, to fall in love only to have it all taken away. Its pain unbearable, echoing into a vast void whose end I cannot fathom. Yet it is that very pain that gives hope, purpose, inspiration – reminds me how sweet and truly beautiful life can be. How lucky I am to have existed at the same time and place as these amazing people. To have lived these now precious memories.

The Cliffs

Here I find myself once more – looking into the endless blue where the sky meets the sea. Cliffs of white topped in a velvety green, dancing in the gale. Peering over an already uncertain ledge, countless stories float, fight, descend, spiral to the rocks below. Relentless waves, far too eager for their next meal. The last time I found myself with legs balanced between the light of day and the night of the Atlantic below, life was at an eerily similar parallel.

For years I had imagined letting go. Embracing what it must feel like to surrender myself to gravity and time. To finally relinquish what little control I believed to have. Yet when the moment came, seated on the white cliffs where countless others before me had made that plunge, I instead found myself enamored with the beauteous gift that has been this life. Instead of joining the other lost souls who cut their stories to an abrupt halt, I found my heart filling with joy. Laughter. Gratitude.

Waves of memories washed over me. A smile so warm I forgot the salted chill billowing from below. Eyes that gleaned bright enough to make the moon blush and hide in envy. A laughter so large, so profound and brimming with life that death itself paused in his tracks to listen. This glow radiating from within. The unfamiliar ember of flickering light against the depths of the unknown. This… hope. The realization that life truly is in the present. Carefully backing away from the ledge of a predetermined fate, enveloped in the warm embrace of uncertainty.

Years later here we are again. Wrapped in life's new weave, the dust of yesterday washed in the river of time. A familiar panic rising in my chest. This pounding rhythm from within… no longer was it my own. A warm regard, a soft look, draped in spontaneity, lost in the lingering taste of a kiss-hat startling realization that my heart no longer belonged to me.

The thought occurs to me now, this time could be different. I could always end it now, prematurely halt what little has begun. The edge is right there and all it would take is one certain step into the finality of all. Accepting one last descent into an all too familiar spiral.

Rather than to feed the waves the despair they so crave, I could stay here. The wind blowing my hair one way and my will another. My heart commanding my feet one way, my mind desperately begging for a semblance of decorum. Frozen in fear and admiration. Embracing the stark reality that for the first time I can recall, I truly want to live. The waves below have lost their siren call, the bottle tasting less sweet, death losing the tenderness of its lullaby. I want to live.

Safely away from the cliffs once more, the dawning of a newfound responsibility pressing me onward – I walk along the path. Faces come and they pass, their gentle smiles, not a soul knowing how close they were to witnessing my end. Not that any of it matters at present—because for the first time I accept the fact I want to live. And that alone is an immeasurable gift I never anticipated receiving.

Grains of Sand

Where the sky meets the land, you'll find me there. Somewhere between the rising moon and the drawing shadows across the sand, draped in the hopes of tomorrow – the flames rise. An all-consuming, overwhelming silence drifts across the dunes, joining us for tea. Wrapped in an embrace as comforting as it is unknown, watching the heavens stare back at us, attempting to quantify the infinite vastness of the unknown – I find myself at home. Finally at peace. I am everything my ancestors couldn't begin to imagine. I am the one clothed in moonlight and taboo, soaking in the mysteries of an arid landscape they've only heard of from the stories of Moses. I am the one surrendering myself to the unknown, communicating in a language older than words. I am the one, arms spread, mouth agape in wonder and joy, dancing beneath the heavens they once revered. I am the one who finally made it home.

The sand sifting between my fingers, each grain a moment frozen in time. Each star, equally dead as it is alive, shining down upon us. Everything a reminder of how truly insignificant we are. And yet, that is the beauty of it all. To count the stars, as is to count the grains of sand, is a task in futility. Just as worthwhile as it would be to count the blades of grass in a meadow. If each of us is a blade of grass, a grain of sand, a drop of water slowly flowing back to its source – truly a wonder in our insignificance.

Sure, on our own we are nothing but a single thread woven into the fabric of time. If we were to step back, to fully witness the beauty of the tapestry that is fate, we could see how each individual thread is woven in its length and how it affects those around it. We could see how that one thread has impacted the entire pattern… simply because of its existence. Each twist, each turn of the weave – our choices impact those around us in this lifetime and those in the lifetimes to come. One grain of sand in the desert may seem like nothing. Despite the appearance of smallness and inconsequence, it could be the very grain that finds itself sifting through your fingers as you contemplate your morality over tea with a practical stranger thousands of miles from home and everything you knew.

Come and dance with me, take my hand. Surrender to the stars above and the sand below. Follow me into the madness that is the human experience and join me in the reverence of the futility of our ambition. Life is too short, too precious to be taken so seriously. If we truly are grains of sand being washed away in the river of time, why is it that we allow ourselves to be so ensnared in our individualism? I accept that I am but a useless grain of sand. Yet when surrendered to love, to community, we insignificant grains form a mighty riverbed that carries the waters of life. Surely one star may shine brighter than another, but each is needed to blanket the night sky in immeasurable beauty.

Where the sky greets the earth, where the sun kisses the horizon at dawn and dusk, you'll find us here. Drinking in the immense nothingness that is divinity. So please, come. Have a seat and make yourself at home. There's a cup waiting just for you.

Sisyphus' Freedom

When the last of the poppy seed has been removed from the pile of earth and ash, when Sisyphus has reached the top of the hill once more, when the moon has set and the stars go to sleep, will the sun be prepared to rise?

Driving his heel, straining, grasping for the motivation to trudge up that hill, Sisyphus has only this moment. This desire to overcome the odds with sheer force, the brutality that is the drive of survival. The will power to see the end and continue pressing on. However, what happens when Sisyphus finally sees dawn's first light? The pinks and oranges gently caressing the edge of the night sky he has always known. Does he keep pressing forward or does he stop and admire the violets he has crushed in his wake, the deep grooves scars from his years of toil?

When the boulder finally rushes past him, outside of his grasp, where is he to go? The illuminated valley below filled with other tortured souls like him, too scared to lift their eyes from their personal hell to notice the brilliance of day. The panic swells in his chest. Should he go chasing after the boulder, placing himself under its weight once more before anyone sees him? He dives to the earth, pressing himself into the ground as much as it would give. Praying maybe if he pressed and writhed hard enough, he would be swallowed into its further depths.

"What am I to do? Where am I to go? I'm not allowed to leave. I'm supposed to stay here. Who else will push the boulder up this hill? Who is going to stop the boulder from crushing the people below? I am a failure. A fraud. An imposter. Aren't I supposed to be the mighty Sisyphus? The one who never tires, never stops, never rests. Only pushes this boulder for all eternity as is my ordained place in this society of the damned."

The questions boil over themselves, engulfing him with their madness. His arms around his knees, he rocks gently on the hillside. Too scared to look, he hears the screams of those being crushed below. He didn't mean for anyone to get hurt. The rocking crescendos to the rhythm of his racing heart. Paralyzed in his panic, he finally drops. Falling back into the well-worn earth beneath him, he dares to open his eyes to the sky. Birds cross, calling to one another, chasing and diving in this beautiful dance he's never seen before. With his eyes to the ground, shoulder into the rock, his reality had been consumed by his duty to the boulder and the souls around him. Now, liberated from his reality, the world slowly comes into vision. The soft grass between his fingers, the breeze carrying away the usual scent of sweat and damnation to introduce new, lighter notes. Of floral, laughter, of joy and perhaps… rose? His mother.

He'd almost forgotten her, these years in hell. The breeze held the faintest trace of her perfume, reminding him of who he was. Who he is. A curious little thing, always chasing after butterflies, the ends of rainbows. He found himself climbing the tallest trees so as to be better positioned to receive every last drop of sunlight before it dipped below the horizon. His mother's voice carrying across the meadow, reminding him it was time to come home. And now, deep in the caverns of hell, she calls him once more. The fleeting trace of her rose scented embrace echo, holding him faster than the weight of any boulder.

Next to him, just outside of the path paved by the boulder, grows a small patch of violets. Perhaps the only ones left unmolested by his years of toil. His mother's voice comes back to him.

"Whenever you are feeling scared, look to the violets. If she allows, take her with you for she is the bringer of good luck. You see my love, the violets were blessed by God. How else could any one creation bring such joy?"

Perhaps for the first time in years, Sisyphus smiled. In taking one delicate purple bloom into his hands, he already felt closer to home and further away from this damnation that he allowed himself to serve for far too long. With lady luck in his pocket, and love in his heart, Sisyphus picked himself from the ground. Filling his lungs to their brim, he was prepared to take the first step of many. It was time to come home.

www.ingramcontent.com/pod-product-compliance
Lightning Source LLC
Chambersburg PA
CBHW020508160726
47991CB00007B/2860